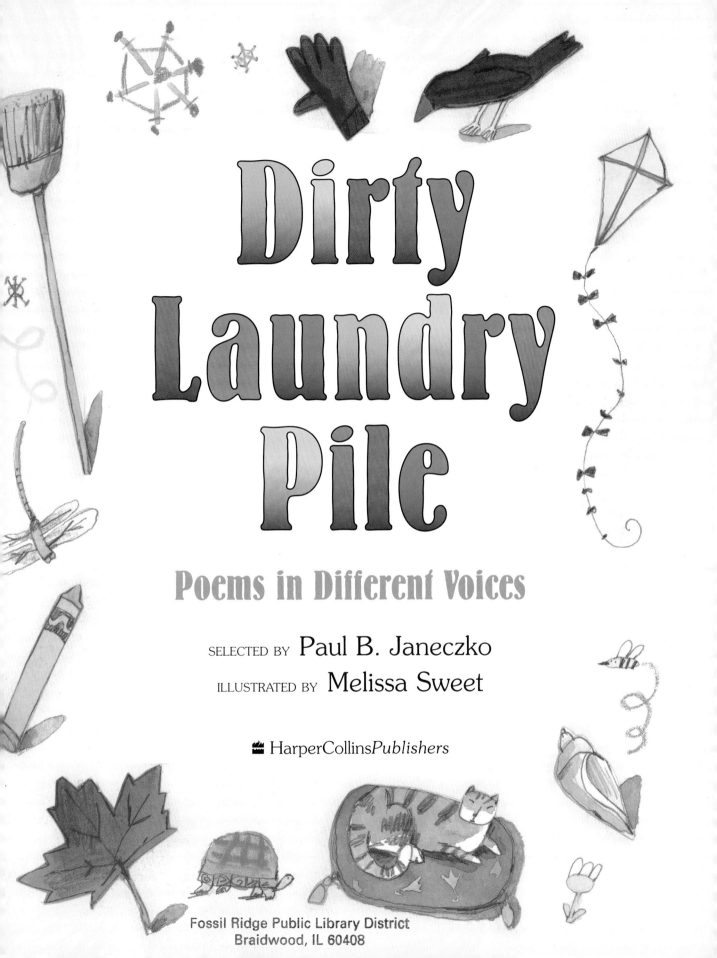

Dirty Laundry Pile

Poems in Different Voices

SELECTED BY Paul B. Janeczko

ILLUSTRATED BY Melissa Sweet

HarperCollins*Publishers*

for Tom Collins,

my friend, not just another pretty face from New Jersey

". . . tramps like us, baby we were born to run" —Bruce Springsteen

—P.J.

To Lisa and Tom

—M.S.

For permission to include poems, we gratefully acknowledge the following:

"Shell," from *Balloons and Other Poems,* by Deborah Chandra. Copyright © 1988, 1990 by Deborah Chandra. Used by permission of Farrar, Straus and Giroux, LLC; "Winter Wind," by Judith Pacht. Copyright © 1998 by Judith Pacht. Reprinted by permission of the author; "Scarecrow's Dream," by Nina Nyhart. From *Openers,* published by Alice James Books. Copyright © 1979. Reprinted by permission of Nina Nyhart; "Prayer of a Snowflake" and "Curtain's Call," by Cynthia Pederson. Copyright © 2001 by Cynthia Pederson. Used by permission of Marian Reiner for the author; "I'm Up Here," copyright © 1972 by Karla Kuskin. Reprinted by permission of S©ott Treimel New York; "Being a Kite," by Jacqueline Sweeney. Copyright © 2001 by Jacqueline Sweeney. Used by permission of Marian Reiner; "Washing Machine," by Bobbi Katz. From *Listen! A Book of Noisy Poems,* by Bobbi Katz, published by Dutton Children's Books. Copyright © 2000 by Bobbi Katz. Used with the permission of Bobbi Katz; "Dirty Laundry Pile," by Marcy Barack Black. Copyright © 2001 by Marcy Barack Black. Used by permission of Marian Reiner; "Broom," by Tony Johnston. Copyright © 2001 by Tony Johnston. Used by permission of the author, who controls all rights; "The Vacuum Cleaner's Revenge," by Patricia Hubbell. Copyright © 2001 by Patricia Hubbell. Used by permission of Marian Reiner; "Crayon Dance," by April Halprin Wayland. Copyright © 2000 by April Halprin Wayland. Used by permission of the author. This poem was first published in the March 2000 issue of *Cricket* magazine; "The Red Gloves," by Siv Cedering. Copyright © 1998 by Siv Cedering. Used by permission of the author; "Old Elm Speaks," by Kristine O'Connell George, from *Old Elm Speaks,* by Kristine O'Connell George. Text copyright © 1998 by Kristine O'Connell George. Reprinted by permission of Clarion Books/Houghton Mifflin Company. All rights reserved; "Roots" and "Old Tortoise," by Madeleine Comora. Used by permission of the author, who controls all rights; "Maple Talk," by Lilian Moore. Reprinted with the permission of Atheneum Books for Young Readers, an imprint of Simon & Schuster Children's Publishing Division, from *Poems Have Roots.* Text copyright © 1997 by Lilian Moore; "Job Satisfaction," by John Collis. From *The Kingfisher Book of Comic Verse,* selected by Roger McGough, published by Kingfisher Books, London, © 1986; "The Mosquito's Song," by Peggy B. Leavitt. Copyright © 2001 by Peggy B. Leavitt. Used by permission of the author; "Plea of the Old Horse on Looking through the Kitchen Window," from *A Grass Green Gallop: Poems by Patricia Hubbell* (Atheneum) © 1990 by Patricia Hubbell. Used by permission of Marian Reiner for the author; "Cat Speak," from *Could We Be Friends? Poems for Pals,* written by Bobbi Katz and illustrated by Joung Un Kim, from Mondo's Bookshop Literacy Program. Text copyright © 1997 by Bobbi Katz, reprinted by permission of Mondo Publishing, One Plaza Road, Greenvale, NY 11548. All rights reserved; "The Prayer of the Cat," from *Prayers from the Ark,* by Carmen Bernos de Gasztold, translated by Rumer Godden, copyright © 1962, renewed 1990 by Rumer Godden. Original copyright 1947, © 1955 by Editions du Cloitre. Used by permission of Viking Penguin, a division of Penguin Putnam Inc.; "Turtle in July," by Marilyn Singer. Reprinted with the permission of Atheneum Books for Young Readers, an imprint of Simon & Schuster Children's Publishing Division, from *Turtle in July,* by Marilyn Singer. Text copyright © 1989 by Marilyn Singer; "Grandpa Bear's Lullaby," by Jane Yolen. Copyright © 1980 by Jane Yolen. First appeared in *Dragon Night and Other Lullabies,* published by Methuen. Reprinted by permission of Curtis Brown, Ltd.; "The Whale," from *Beast Feast,* copyright © 1994 by Douglas Florian, reprinted by permission of Harcourt, Inc.; "The Cow's Complaint," from *How Now, Brown Cow?* Text copyright © 1994 by Alice Schertle, reprinted by permission of Harcourt, Inc.; "Hippopotamus," by Ronald Wallace. From *Plums, Stones, Fishes, and Hooks,* University of Missouri Press. Copyright © 1981 by Ronald Wallace. Reprinted by permission of the author.

Library of Congress Cataloging-in-Publication Data
Dirty laundry pile : poems in different voices / selected by Paul B. Janeczko ; illustrated by Melissa Sweet.
p.   cm.
Summary: A scarecrow, washing machine, cow, and other objects and animals express themselves in this collection of poems.
ISBN 0-688-16251-7 — ISBN 0-688-16252-5 (lib. bdg.)
1. Children's poetry, American.   [1. American poetry—Collections.]   I. Janeczko, Paul B.   II. Sweet, Melissa, ill.
PS586.3 .D57   2001   00-26857
811.008'09282—dc21

1   2   3   4   5   6   7   8   9   10   ❖   First Edition

Introduction

I collected the poems in this book because I love reading poems written in the voice of an object or an animal, as if that thing or creature were speaking to me. In these persona or mask poems, as they are called, the poets let their imaginations fly and feel what it might be like to be a mosquito, a crayon, a kite, a turtle. It's something like wearing a Halloween costume or playing a part in a school play. Great fun, don't you think? As you read these poems, if you find yourself wondering what it would feel like to be a caterpillar, a soccer ball, or a honeybee, grab a pencil and let *your* imagination fly in a poem.

Let that new voice sing!

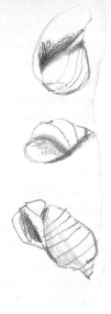

Shell Deborah Chandra

Come, press my mouth against your ear,
I hold a message just for you,
Deep inside my throat is where
It curls, waiting for you to hear.

Put there by the sea itself,
Who whispered something you should know
In shadowy sounds wound round my shell,
And with my hidden tongue, I'll tell.

Winter Wind   Judith Pacht

Through cracks and holes I bore
then glide along the floor
looking for your knees and wrists
(necks and arms are on my list).
I'm winter wind shaking the door
with both my fists.

When circling to play
I blow cold gusts your way
but all you do is stay in bed
or bundle up, sip soup instead.
Okay, then stay. I'll sweep away.
There's snow ahead.

Scarecrow's Dream Nina Nyhart

I think it's June—
crows landing in black waves.

Farmer arrives with his .22.
Stop, I say. And put away

that gun, I'll handle this.
Farmer shrugs, strides off.

For once I'm boss, and we're
a circle of friends. We discuss,

make deals: a little corn—
a little reticence. Come at night—

save your life. Peaceable
kingdom I'm thinking when

I feel a step on my shoulder,
the first peck in my eye.

Prayer of a Snowflake Cynthia Pederson

Let me land, oh Lord,

on a narrow needle of pine,

or a sheltered slope

where I can memorize

the trim track of a passing fox.

I want more

than a month before melting.

If I can't have

that long, quiet life,

grant me a sledded slope.

Or better yet, I hope

for my swirling journey to end instantly

on the hot tongue

of some shivering child

out reveling in the return

of my tribe.

Amen.

I'm Up Here
Karla Kuskin

I'm up here.

You're down there.

And nothing in that space between us

But a mile of air.

Where I sail:

Clouds pass.

Where you run:

Green grass.

Where I float:

Birds sing.

One thin thing there is

That holds us close together:

Kite string.

Being a Kite   Jacqueline Sweeney

If I were a kite
I'd kneel,
stretch my skinny arms
out wide,
and wait for wind.

My yellow shirt would
fill up like a sail
and flap,
tugging my criss-crossed
wooden bones and me
towards seas of cloud.

My rippling paper skin
would rustle like applause
as I inhaled,
gulping one last gust
to swoop me giddy-quick
above the trees.

My red rag tail
would drift
toward everything green
to balance me

so all day

I could loop and climb
loop and climb
and soar
into pure sky.

Washing Machine   Bobbi Katz

I'm the washing machine.
I make dirty clothes clean,
so that nobody has to rub:

Glubita   glubita
glubita
glubita   glubita

glubita . . .

GLUB.

Swizzle-dee-swash—
Swizzle-dee-swash—

I talk to myself,
while I do the wash!

Babba-da-swaba—

I change my song
as the cycle moves along.
Soapsuds gurgle through my hose.
Then . . .

Blub-blub-a-dubba—
I rinse the clothes.

Blippety-blop— blippety-blop—
I spin,
spin, spin

and then . . .
I stop.

Dirty Laundry Pile
Marcy Barack Black

Ignore me now
On the floor
By the door.
But you'll notice
When I swell
By my smell.

Broom Tony Johnston

I am the trusted consort
of floors, accomplice
of water and swash,
confidant of corners
where skulks shifty, fugitive
trash.
I am blunt whisker,
ghost-voiced shadow-sweeper
(suspicious of the dark),
collector of exquisite
scraps,
confessor to expiring
flies,
seeker-of-the-lost,
keeper-of-the-uncherished,
the crushed.
I share the deepest secrets
of the dust.

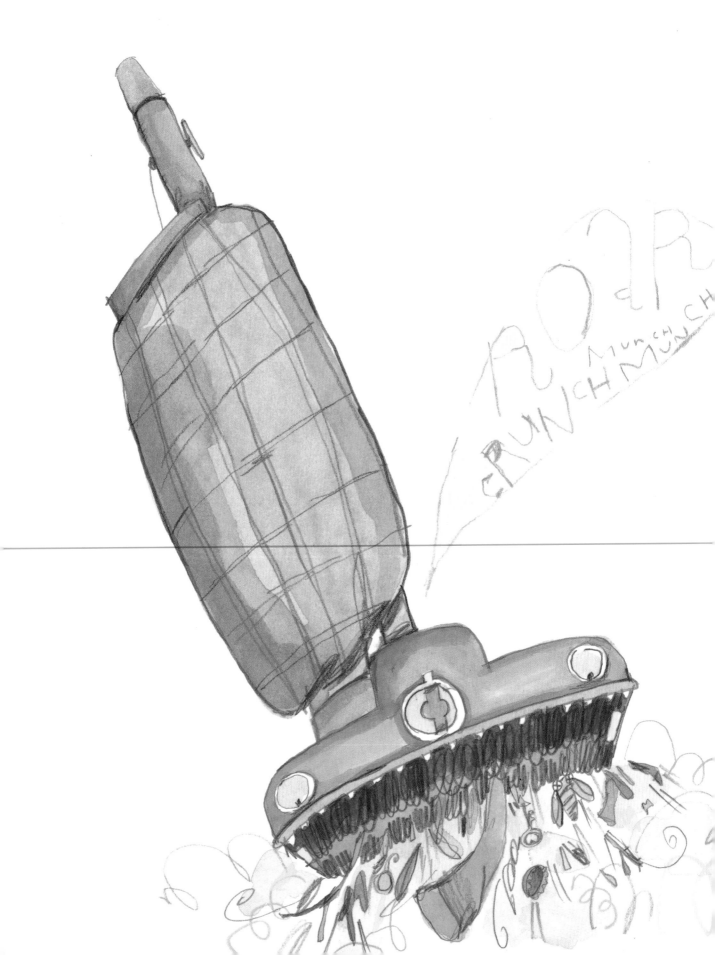

The Vacuum Cleaner's Revenge
Patricia Hubbell

I munch. I crunch.
I zoom. I roar.

I clatter-clack
Across the floor.

I swallow twigs.
I slurp dead bugs.

I suck the cat hair
From the rugs.

My stomach full
Of dirt and dust

I gulp another
Pizza crust.

A tiresome life—
All work, no play—

I think I'll swallow *you* today!

Crayon Dance April Halprin Wayland

The cardboard ceiling lifts
Pickmepickmepickme, I pray
The fingers do! They choose *me,* Sky Blue!
Hurrah! Hooray!

As I am picked from the pocket
All colors whisper, "Good-bye, Pastel!
Be strong! Don't break!
Enjoy! Farewell!"

Hi, hi! I'm scrubbing a sky!
Some stripes and whorls and—whee!
Cha-cha-cha, loop-de-loop
I'm leaving bits of me!

They gave me a chance!
All of me rocks in this
Fine, wild dance—
The dance of me, Sky Blue!

Leaping and laughing, this message I'm leaving:

Ha ha!

Hi hi!

Hurrah!

Hooray!

. . . Good-bye!

The Red Gloves   Siv Cedering

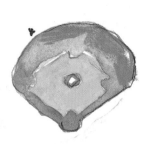

Hey, you forgot us!
Hurry back.

You will find one of us
behind the baseball diamond,
the other one
by the swing.

Without your hands,
we are five-room houses
waiting for our inhabitants
to come home.

We are soft shells
that miss
the snails that would give them
their own slow
speed.

We are red wings
that have forgotten
how to fly.

When you find us,
put us on,

for like puppies who warm each other
all night
you will warm us
and we will warm
your hands

which must be
lost
valentines
without their red
envelopes.

Old Elm Speaks   Kristine O'Connell George

It is as I told you, Young Sapling.

It will take
autumns of patience
before you snag
your
first

moon.

Roots — Madeleine Comora

Roots like ours,
coarse and strong
as a grandmother's fingers,
reach into the earth.
A tangled weave,
rough and aged
like wooden lace.
Roots like ours
hold the world
in place.

Maple Talk Lilian Moore

Plant us.
Let our roots go
deeply down.
We'll hold the soil
when rain tugs
at the earth.

Plant us.
You will better know
how seasons come
and go.

Watch for
    our leaves unfurling
    in spring green,

    our leafy roofs of summer
    over pools of shade,

    our sunset red and gold
    igniting autumn's blaze.

When cold winds
leave us bare
we'll show you treetop nests
where songbirds hid
their young.

And when
in early spring
the sweet sap flows again,
have syrup for your pancakes!

Plant us.

Job Satisfaction — John Collis

I am a young bacterium
And I enjoy my work
I snuggle into people's food
I lie in wait—I lurk.
They chomp a bit and chew a bit
And say, "This can't be beaten"
But then in bed they groan and moan,
"I wish I hadn't eaten."

The Mosquito's Song   Peggy B. Leavitt

I sing.   You slap.

I mean   no harm.

There is no cause

for your alarm.

A little drop

is all I ask.

It really is

a simple task.

So please

hold still

at this

juncture,

while I

make

a tiny

P
U
N
C
T
U
R
E
!

Plea of the Old Horse on Looking through the Kitchen Window
Patricia Hubbell

I have shed my winter coat
and you have not blanketed me—

a warm spell in early March—
I shed too early.

It is cold in the barn now.
Dampness climbs into my ears.

I am shivering, Miss.
Come, and blanket me.

If you will not blanket me,
Will you bring me a carrot?

I see you through the window,
warm at your stove.

I see the carrots.
Won't you come, please, Miss,

Come to blanket me?
Come with a carrot?

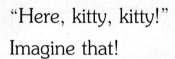

Cat Speak Bobbi Katz

"Here, kitty, kitty!"
Imagine that!
Where did *they* learn to speak to a cat?
Annoying me while I'm taking my ease
in my blue comfy chair in the sun,
if you please.
Annoying me when I'm taking a nap!
Picking me up to plop on a lap!
They have things in a terrible muddle.
I'll decide with whom I'll cuddle.
Perhaps I'll let them stroke my fur,
and when *I* wish, perhaps I'll purr.
Perhaps I'll brush against a leg.
But I give the orders, and *I* don't beg.

The Prayer of the Cat
Carmen Bernos de Gasztold

Lord,

I am the cat.

It is not, exactly,

that I have something to ask of You!

No—

I ask nothing of anyone—

but,

if You have by some chance,

in some celestial barn,

a little white mouse,

or a saucer of milk,

I know someone who would relish them.

Wouldn't You like someday

to put a curse on the whole race of dogs?

If so I should say,

Amen

Old Tortoise
Madeleine Comora

Some might mistake me
for a rock
and pass me in a hurry,
but if you are as slow as I,
you too may touch the grass
and hear it talk all afternoon
and watch and smell and wonder,
"What was that and that and that?"
Listen as the trees reach high.
Their leaves are softly singing.
Hold your ear close to the ground—then wait.
You may just hear the old rocks breathe.

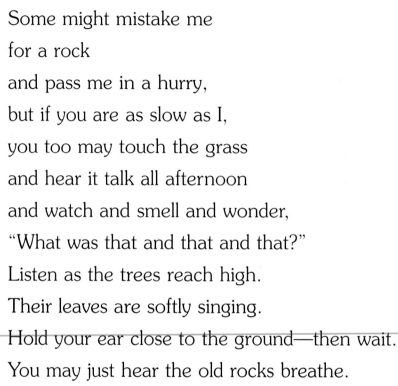

Turtle in July
Marilyn Singer

Heavy

Heavy hot

Heavy hot hangs

Thick sticky

Icky

But I lie

Nose high

Cool pool

No fool

A turtle in July

Grandpa Bear's Lullaby
Jane Yolen

The night is long
But fur is deep.
You will be warm
In winter sleep.

The food is gone
But dreams are sweet
And they will be
Your winter meat.

The cave is dark
But dreams are bright
And they will serve
As winter light.

Sleep, my little cubs, sleep.

The Whale
Douglas Florian

Big as a street—

With fins, not feet—

I'm full of blubber,

With skin like rubber.

When I breathe out,

I spew a spout.

I swim by the shore

And eat more and more.

I'm very, very hard to ignore.

The Cow's Complaint
Alice Schertle

How unkind to keep me here
When, over there, the grass is greener.
Tender blades—so far, so near—
How unkind to keep me here!
Through this fence they make me peer
At sweeter stems; what could be meaner?
How unkind to keep me here
When, over there, the grass is greener.

Hippopotamus Ronald Wallace

I am tired of wallowing
in this mud and my own hide.
If I were a poet,
and not a hippopotamus,
I could be anything I wanted.
A gazelle, for instance.
The word springs from my mouth,
grows graceful
legs and muscles:
gazelle, gazelle,
it dances on its syllables.
Excited by flies,
I waddle over to my thick wife,
full of the secrets of poetry.

Curtain's Call
Cynthia Pederson

I clap them awake
   on summer days
with a wink of wide-eyed light.

I swell them to sleep
   on wind-whittled nights
when my white wings lift
   into warm starlight.

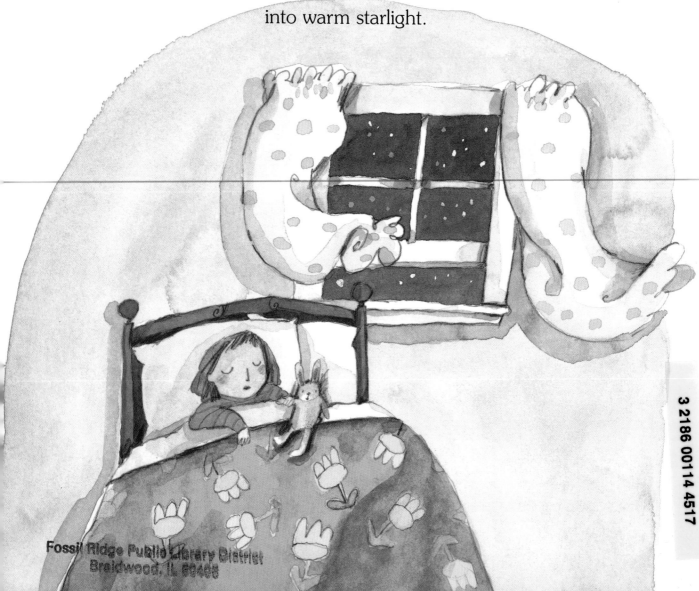